Pastels Are Pretty Much the Polar Opposite of Chalk

By the Same Author

Bowlbrawl
Let's Pretend We Never Met
Wrong Bar

NATHANIEL G. MOORE

Pastels Are Pretty Much the Polar Opposite of Chalk

LIVRES DC BOOKS

Cover art by Kelly Schykulski, colagene.com.
Author photograph by Mary Williamson.
Book designed and typeset by Primeau Barey, Montreal.
Edited by Jason Camlot for the Punchy Writers Series.

Copyright © Nathaniel G. Moore, 2009.
Legal Deposit, Bibliothèque et Archives nationales du Québec
and the National Library of Canada, 4th trimester, 2009.

Library and Archives Canada Cataloguing in Publication
Moore, Nathaniel G
Pastels are pretty much the polar opposite of chalk / Nathaniel G. Moore.
(Punchy poetry)
ISBN 978-1-897190-58-6 (bound).
ISBN 978-1-897190-57-9 (pbk.)
I. Title. II. Series: Punchy poetry
PS8626.O595P38 2009   C811'.6   C2009-905957-6

This is a work of art. Names, characters, places, and events are either products
of the author's imagination or are employed fictitiously. Any resemblance to actual
events or locales or persons, living or dead, is entirely coincidental.

No part of this publication may be reproduced or stored in a retrieval system
or transmitted in any form or by any means, electronic, mechanical, recording,
or otherwise, without written permission of the publisher, DC Books.

In the case of photocopying or other reprographic copying, a license must be
obtained from Access Copyright, Canadian Copyright Licensing Agency,
1 Yonge Street, Suite 800, Toronto, Ontario M5E 1E5 <info@accesscopyright.ca>

For our publishing activities, DC Books gratefully acknowledges the financial
support of the Canada Council for the Arts, of SODEC, and of the Government
of Canada through the Book Publishing Industry Development Program (BPIDP).

Canada Council for the Arts   **Conseil des Arts du Canada**

Société de développement des entreprises culturelles
Québec

Printed and bound in Canada by Groupe Transcontinental. Interior pages
printed on 100 per cent recycled and FSC certified Enviro Print white paper.
Distributed by LitDistCo.

Mixed Sources
Product group from well-managed forests,
controlled sources and recycled wood or fiber
www.fsc.org Cert no. SW-COC-000952
© 1996 Forest Stewardship Council
FSC

DC Books
PO Box 666, Station Saint-Laurent
Montreal, Quebec H4L 4V9
www.dcbooks.ca

Contents

Part 1: Leopard Frog

- 3 Pigment Juice
- 4 Just too Simple
- 5 Too Simple II
- 6 December Rain
- 8 Donlands Avenue
- 9 A Lamp in His Room
- 11 Pastels Are Pretty Much the Polar Opposite of Chalk
- 16 Spiders Fraud Mars
- 20 I'm Going to Sour, Are You?
- 21 The Pelican
- 23 Quick, Slippery Eels
- 24 In the Garden Using My Books

Part 2: Pyromania

- 28 Velcro to Lavender to Dusk Cake
- 30 Pyromania
- 31 Planet 9
- 34 A Rasp Carpology
- 35 The Hospital Is for Sick Children
- 36 All Childhood Accidents (and) Injuries I Experienced
- 37 Just for One Moment
- 38 Just Hold On a Second: It's 8:17 p.m. EST.
- 39 Just for a Single Moment
- 40 10 Things I Know About Toronto for a Fact
- 41 The Julia Stiles Banquet Face-Fetish Club
- 42 "Emily"

46 Fabrication Land
47 Vinegar
48 Clockers
49 Wrong Way to Tinsel
50 The Cashier Isn't Always This Slow
56 "The 10 Things I Am Going to Eat off Your Plate."
57 "It's 1880s Night. You Look like a Slut."
58 I Have Eaten the Oil Painting Which You Left on My Wall
59 Small House

Part 3: An Effort Which Does Not Pay

63 Smaller Narrative
65 The Evaluation of a Patient with Abdominal Pain by a Bus Driver
66 Parsley
67 Pelvic Mascara Marking
69 Thieves Like Us
70 Use Weasel Phrases Megan, It's Your Turn
71 Werewolf Tumour
73 That's My Brother, Jawa
74 Arugula Wasted
79 Acknowledgements

Part 1:
Leopard Frog

Pigment Juice

Who has promised us
a new flavour,

yet delivered nicotine?
Who has made us addictive and boring?

Xerox.
Xerox did it.

Xerox ordered my heart:
Like a constellation we pose for.

Like a news hour, chafing the crew.
Like gold grinning at a tin-tortured sun.

Like all these similes.
I am an imposition, one pigment at a time.

Just too Simple

The phone is brown.
The goat is cold.

The swan is gold.
The damn is loud.

I haven't heard from you in a while.
"Listen to me.

You never listen to me. You have a complex
dark side but your other side is just too simple.

I get so bored."
The porn is racist.

The goat is moldy.
The swamp is cold.

The lard is damned.
Sound leaks from a twinkling larynx.

A larynx is a lot like a dutiful
constellation.

Too Simple II

Stellar in size and potency,
two large spaces cluster.

When lines are added they form a leaning
rectangle, angled left.

The angle leaves.
The angle has left the building.

The afternoon is late.
The snow has completely thawed.

The remains are skeletal.
Slush sleeps in polar bears.

The Big Dipper has crashed asteroids.
Clumps of nutrients follicle each other around.

But from here we just say something sharp
so to puncture the crooked rural sky.

December Rain

Many years from now.
For weeks it rained tinsel slowly.
I was a poor flower girl selling petunias

on the boardwalk, my sneakers set to cling
on the side of a curdled asteroid.
Just like in the past poem.

My indoor pages however had not yet been written.
I was arthritic. Eventually I sold enough flowers.
As you can see by the catalogue copy frozen to Aunt Julia's mittens:

In these classic
poems of low-octane
sweet menace, the poet
has layered the souls of those aged
seventeen to seventy who stalked
tawdry boardwalks with apathy.

Layer-bears laid bear-sauced apple faces.
Mouths were paced with digestive breaks.
Those aged one-o-one were declared naturally un-fun.

The poet said, not in so many words, "We'll see."
Things took place quickly in those days.
There was talk of winter insects withstanding traditional deaths.

Air curdled as the mellow hornet wept
and his gelatin eyes told the whole story to each marigold.
And it made sense?

To each old fat neighbour beating their laundry dry?
To each old fat neighbourhood bus beating its lights?
To each hiss?

To each blood cell worth its Christmas salt.
To each hissing bear
        asking goodnight.

"Goodnight?"

        Goodnight, many years from now.

Donlands Avenue

The clock is still 3:38 p.m., has been since I ever
saw it in 1986, since I ever land-marked it.
Every bus transfer has been used to papier-mache
my face, making me permanently weak.
Jumping through sprinklers on Church fronts
at Cosburn intersection:
A blissful memory blade of infinite grass.

A Lamp in His Room

The neighbourhood is an even charge
                of muted browns
                        and greens.

The soil is firm, wet; the knitted grass
      is matted down.

A hope for real texture, form or sway
        gristles as early spring listens.

These two voices mutter in low decibels:
"Are we growing, to be pulled, trodden, or burned?"

All this is months away. Time's cloud forms slowly.

"When we're together it's like,
Oh God, he just wants me to be a lamp in his room."

[The poem voice is low decibel, brittle, accurate]:
Put your head on my toilet,
on my cold cold toilet.

My closed cold toilet
that is a display toilet
in a model home.

Rest on it your head gentle and calm.

"Don't be annoying. That is exactly how it is
when we're together. I think to myself, 'Well
I can do his laundry in a crazy outfit,

and that's the extent of my freedom, the only
way it can be expressed.'"

All this is months away.

And so around your head unpredictable
orbits in porcelain
the most demented halo.

I wish you an evening of green tidal waves,
                                          or brown.

And my crazy-assed outfit.
And my fakie whimpers.
Baby talk is the extent of my freedom,
and the only dead star is roughed up
like a dirty girl carpet burn.

Pastels Are Pretty Much the Polar Opposite of Chalk

Pastels are pretty much the polar opposite of chalk.
I like anything that creates dust.
Whether it's "Chalk pastel" or not, it's still chalk.
But that's like saying:

"Oh, a leopard frog is still a leopard."
No, no it's not.

And yes, I have used them. Clearly–chalk pastels,
I mean–not leopard
frogs.

Do I like pretzels/hard pretzels? Do I prefer the small ones
or the giant squishy ones?

Those traditionally twisted into an Orthodox knot.
The noun pastel gives rise to another noun,

for an artwork whose medium is pastels, a verb,
meaning, to produce an artwork with pastels,
an adjective,

meaning pale in color.

Twisted into an Orthodontist knot, inside a leopard's soft
spotted jaw, the baked bread with branded salt deposits
comes in a variety of shapes and conditions minted
 by the foul-beaked Mugwamps of Kingston.

Who examines each inch of twist? They do: the *Orthodon-tistrists*.

You are looking for flaws and when you cannot find

legitimate ones you make them up and hope that
I'll be convinced. You are like a warranty,
or a warrant, or a cold blooded rant.

No one thinks I appear hostile but you.
I'm thinking about the rest-home hostility.
You're a lunatic.

I keep tabs on you
car chase after car chase.

Car chase often describes the pursuit of a criminal
by police, increasingly captured on film from media
or police systems of capture.

The captor's ligament or ligaments, twisted in a breeze
of steps, squats, hesitation and sudden sidewalk adjustments
make pretzel criminality.

"I like pastels. I guess I like things done
in pastels as long as I don't have to touch them."

I pelted nothing, no parchment or tendon. I made no
impression thinking: as long as it's not me at the pastel
wheel,

so brilliant, bold, covered in dust and gold. I touched no
pastel, drove no car, stroked neither leopard nor spot.

At least I am not using the typing hand
I want to wed.

It is free to dangle, to type, to be on its

own not touching the me key or the chalk.

Not wiping a nearby mouth.
Not pending the narrow jaw of a hurtled pose.

The blur of my eyelids in the pastel tense has a dramatic fit.
My mouth is outlined in *cough-chalk* time lines.

A voice is brittle.
A tone is brutal.

"You see, I don't mess with them much myself,
they're not really my thing. Too messy.
Here you go: *why do you ask?*"

Question: What is the meaning of a stick, consisting of pure powdered pigment,

and a binder?

And.

"What about car chases? Watching
them or being in them?"

You, my dear, are the car chase I can't afford to choreograph.
The pastel draft that makes me cough the most.

I am not really my thing really.
No, you are not really your thing.
Yes, you are not really my thing.

And I sang, even though I did not understand a word I sang:

"oh a leopard frog is still a leopard."
"oh a leopard frog is still a leopard."

"oh a leopard frog is still a leopard."
"oh a   ."

"oh a leopard frog is still a leopard."
"oh a leopard frog is still a leotard."

"oh a leopard frog is still a leopard."
"oh a leopard frog is still a leopard."

"oh a leopard frog is still a leopard."

Spiders Fraud Mars

Before all this happened on May 13th 1987,
when all this happened on May 13th 1987,
can you believe this happened?

Julia and I worked for Mars Tours for four weeks.
        (March 13, 1987–April 10, 1987)

"One day [May 13, 1987] it consumed us [Julia and I],"
   I told *Redbook*.

We were strolling on a beach of vacation points.

"The pamphlet, remember all the typos in the pamphlet!"
   Julia said.
"Managers can be like that, all toxic, all quicksand,
   no gladness." I replied.

We both knew the slogan so well. [MARS TOURS:
   Like our name, arachnids a given.]

   We had eschewed the beach crowd and vipered through
   a nice ankle tangle [weedy trail 300 feet from the ocean]
   passing a one-legged
   pirate popping bite-sized urchins from sandblasted fists
   past an eye-patched mouth.
   His golden peg gleamed in the sunlight–

"Seared at our migraines," Julia told *The Times*.

But really it was the netting,
webbing each of our bodies in a Stocking of Truth.

"We were soon to be dissected like
students in a pupa state," I told *Esquire*.

Julia was moaning from her "Esophagus of truth creams"
    saying she knew
this was going to happen because of her truth creams.
"Can you reach my army knife?" I asked.

Our exposed diamonds of skin ovened like protein.
We became an impromptu meal for the Goliath Tarantula
    of the coastal rain
forests of Northeastern S. America.

"Can't reach it," Julia said.

In the jungle–
"The mighty jungle?" *People* asked–

I saw this big ape spider performing at top speed
with is radial saws.
I admired his acclaimed eight-legged show.

His poison perfumed our wounds,
embalmed our sighs.

"I urge you Jules, reach forth through the web of truths and friction,
and maybe we can break this clasp trap."

Then. Swelling, mild pain, sweat, silver, gold, a big spider coma. "Eurethromycin," I cooed.

"I think he's coming back" Julia said.

Then, in the nest, Julia cooed,
and passed me the self-defense pamphlet.
"As you can see, they don't always contain words,"
she said.
I looked at her red swollen fingers.

"Have I told you the story of when I fell in love with you?"
I asked.

We cocooned like little lovers,
nested like turtle doves,
and made intimate little guesses
at whose legs were to go next.

I'm Going to Sour, Are You?

Tetherballed in repetition,
rope-flying in the boring night,
I board a flight.

I move to Sour
and murmur in heatstroke
until unlit lake-dip bliss finds me.

"I hold you."
"I feel the same."
"I rest my head."
"I mine the whole planet."
"I like just you."

We move to Sour
(a town in Southwest Lebanon
80 km/50 miles south of Beirut).

"Look we've worn things down to cud,
the calf, the curb. Our last meal worming
like slippery eels in the boring night."

You can find us in Sour,
murmuring in heatstroke,
nude until unlit lake-dip bliss finds us.

Still in Sour,
tether-balled in repetition,
rope-flying in the boring night.

The Pelican

When someone suggests spaghetti, it is never good news. As
 Snagglepuss, you can be all pink
and randy, a bit of a dandy. But never do you want to watch
 someone cook spaghetti. It's like watching a crime show
 reenactment: Then s/he made spaghetti.

Oh, it's usually the late afternoon, and for some, the day's
 coldest hour.

You can distract them with thoughtful banter, designed to
 compromise their sense of originality.
You can go on and on for the poem's sake!

"Do they sell that at the grocery store?
And is there more than one package?

Remember the next two Bond films have carbo-load themes
 that gnaw on two main points:
Spaghetti is temporary. Diamonds are forever."

You can get international, psychiatric, automotive even!

"Spaghetti is often a metaphor for sunsets, hooo-lll-ahhh-
 tics (the art of grass skirt) and a dormant pallet. In some
 countries, bits of spaghetti are chewed or crushed into
 small sizes and used in pellet guns for war-torn children's
 day programs."

Or nature programs! Everyone loves animals. Do that! Talk
 about animals using spaghetti in interesting ways!

"Also, pelicans use spaghetti as a symbol of strand pride. The
 pelican with the hottest strand is considered the wisest.
 Although the pelicans have no ability to cook the food,

their ability to snatch a single strand is a known marvel."

So now it is time to wrap things up, you know, for the poem's sake.

"So sometimes there will be six pelicans, each with a strand and they all lay 'em out like they are building a nest. And the one with the most steamy strand, well that is the wisest pelican. Then I put that one in the pot and finish the sauce. That one strand. Not that one pelican.

Then I eat the steamy spaghetti and watch my nature poems live on TV."

Quick, Slippery Eels

Our last meal worming
like slippery eels in the boring night,
working their greasy ignorant ways
into our iron stomachs.

Quick, slippery eels.

In the Garden Using My Books

1.

We ate meat on our first date
and kissed bisons
which were axed red.
We used dental floss
which was a private act.

Our red gums took place
behind closed doors.

We all lived in a bungalow.
We all missed the medicine cabinet.
We missed the rusty medicine cabinet.

2.

The nightingale is singing.
The postman is ringing.
The crime novel is reading.
The bird is hitting the window.
The kitchen window is dying.
The Life Network is expensive.

3.

And now I'm in the garden using my books!

I can see the house killing things accidentally
from the lawn where I'm sitting.

Another bird hits the kitchen window.
Sometimes you forget to walk on your toes.
Nutrients move firmly towards the liquoring.

From where I'm sitting I can see
that my sister's room is lacquering.

Magenta.
Pigment.
Magenta.
Magenta.

Hence, I know exactly how to colour the bedroom of
    judgment day (if asked).
Hip-flasked, I know exactly how to colour the powder
    room of judgment day.

We ate meat.
We kissed bisons.
We were lapsed juggernauts
in the service of red charges.

magenta magenta

magenta

Part 2:
Pyromania

Velcro to Lavender to Dusk Cake

To mouth.

I gamble on porno for halos,
for winos and leg rolls.
The sea is my sheet. I grandfather
clock her in the hallway against

the bedpost. I boot her hard. I am not
idle. I stretch. I shadow-drag. I shadow-smear.
I render hard *my my my* jaw. She boxes *me me me.*
And tongue bludgeons *me.* A knee. Then *she,* oh then

she escape-pods Air Force One. She sheets me in

the mouth.

Lots of almonds are in the cake. Lots of mouths are in the dust.
Lots of almonds are covered in the dusk of the mouth.

And Goo.

Her lies perjured comfort food.

Is a Goo centre, jam?
Sure. But the surface is very asteroid,
very ash fault lips,
very Pompeii & Circumstance.

The dust would come later in the digestive sect.
Like excommunicated members of the angry Frankenstein
    farm tool crowd.

She mouth-solves the tinder cake.
With no idleness, but with cake un-tethered by tongue,
    and evil-gazed,
we mouth the solvent blur tinder cake home.

I cave in her cave girl mouth. My male mouth wheels.
She rips skin akin to a taste bud syncing.

We did not hear a Velcro tear all weekend.
My arid cave girl, known for her pirate fort-making
    abilities, her
appreciation of the word pickle. Dynamite. Sure!
We were working hard nailing and finishing.

The flower wet, I am watching it wed air, and hearing
it make an allergic home in the septum of her tiny legs.

Anecdotes gnash hard against the dead rat heart bone
I'm softening up for madness. I am waiting to be guillotined
by the Tonka truck. Choked buy the tire fire in a perilous
    flashback
sequence. A Kodak Christmas paper cut rewrapped,

resurrected, re-gifted. Photo albums
of dead cats, dogs and Uncle Tim.
Now that you are clothed and still
not related to me, I can update the family album:

"Tim was red.
He ate pins."

Pyromania

On Through the Night!

Deceive the sky with aromas
from your magic ovens!

Gather kindling. Let us siphon kerosene gravy.

O Beautiful kite wound. You are tangled in porno reels
and edited-out splices. I tossed you out
the window on a windy day in 1982
and my eye cut open.
O kite wound, I surrender to you and to the sex-frost
beneath my breath
as dawn undoes its fragile dress.
Something hovers over the flames–

Is it a believing or a living ability?

Her thong still sleeps in the throats of clergymen.
Her poems still sleep in the throats of gym class.

She is two very different people
who never existed.

But tonight,
as aromas are heated, as orange licks black,
let us open our wrists on this fanged décor,
and admire your sex-strung face
sprinkled with disease.

Let's float a lonely kite and admire
the flitting tail of sparkling celluloid.

Planet 9

1. Barrels of mischief

"P" moves from one
marooned perching
to the next. Her face is
eating steel. Her fat lips
are eating ice cubes. In
bed she is crying ice tears.

2. Borrowing trouble

Married men stay in
bed. Fast forward through
the playbook. "P" centrefolds
herself. Avoids low watt paper cuts.
But intercourse good.

3. Accelerate the hymns

to include a chorus on
"voice-over blessings,"
"pedestrian verbal
waste management,"
"piggybank underwriting
insurance."

"P" is bored. Launches a nuclear attack.
Swish, missile, swish!
(This is how it sounds
on a vernacular disaster movie set.)

4. Day 17, the script changed? Yeah? Pages 47-on....

Industrialization caved in and spoiled
a few rocks, some dirt and space:
the bear, the fig, the missile too.

A stadium of sunstroke jawbreakers.
A tree is just as populated.
Air just as aggressive,
just as uprooted.

"P" flaunts the cult of lake habits.
"P" warbles and tightropes across a floating log.
"P" flaunts each trout, reaches the phantom quota
with her arms full of dying fish.

"P" goes on and on, "The fish was this
big, believe!"

"P" knows to flaunt is in season.
"P" is freckled, and
is both green
and black.

"P" tipped the canoe into a jar as
the gammy waitress spat a small pencil
through the oars.

"P" goes, "One of us was terrified,
one of us was in the washroom!"

Sometimes we order correctly.
The menus are always brand new.

Sometimes its fingers are depressed.
"Swish missile, swish!"

A Rasp Carpology

I love to visit the Lake of Fire.
I love its casserole-heartburn desire.

The mint green lake is a dull silver beast.
It creases the surface, rasps against

each meek wave while
a flint spark lighter works by

a flint. I will have you know
that ledge after ledge

on the boat a carp is under,
and rapidly bumping the aluminum tub,

you should continue
your quest for fire.

On a mint green lake,
which is a dull silver beast,

I hold a small piece of Ferrocerium.
I have the ability to give

a large number of sparks when
I am scraped against a rough surface,
[pyrophoricity]

against a rough steel surface,
against a rough and lonely place.

Against a rough sea's surface, against a lonely place,
against all odds: The Gaming Commission.

The Hospital Is for Sick Children

Defibrillators double
as harmonicas.

Gurneys eek,
wheezing in and out.

I lean in to love,
reach octaves honestly

without earth's degrading
expectations.

This is a formulated policy
for a dimly lit ruby

covered in water,
in violent water,

that is to say,
in acuity.

Each suture heads south
intent on securing a permanent mood.

Haldol is scuffed up
in a fuzzy EmergRoom.

The following are the real
seasons: Winter. Spring.

Spring2. Summer.
Fall. Fall2.

All Childhood Accidents (and) Injuries I Experienced

The jar full of goose grease from New Year's dinner 1975 was in my way so I moved it with my lemon weak hands seventeen months old playing with paint tins and glass jars

pupil o pupil here you go splat glass edgy on the tightrope burn through the right pupil and everything became disordered a new order forever the balancing act now impossible the brain signals converging

spilling over lopsided a lobotomy of the eye, advancing condensing on the side of my shivering horror-show skull. I mean temple.

Then running into a pole two years on; third eye blind and twice removed, a terrible sequel accident; sequined in twitching stitches on my side watching the needle in and out of my

forensic forehead.

Trying to roller skate in French, (Quebec City) nervously six years later from forehead pow falling unable to syntax or translate
pain properly and the photocopier of an X-ray machine in Quebec not doing its job or doing its job

terribly lamely. Catching a football the next year in phys ed class. Sign my cast of chaos please class? They did.

Just for One Moment

Hey. She's setting the table; it's a single turtleneck moment.

Whenever I think "The way we were...."
I can see our elegiac faces, trembling before

God's photographic spasms like we're looking
at a large golden chest being opened.

Many coins are in the mouth of a *Golden Flint*.
What is a Golden Flint?

It's a type of bird, very rare, who specializes in ESP–
education and administration, very big in Detroit.

Large as some car parts, the pot you cook it in
is like a copper coffin,

of tempura mental, or,
tempered metal.

Let it soak in its red, gold
and copper juices.

Set the table.
Wear a single turtleneck.

Just Hold On a Second: It's 8:17 p.m. EST.

The airport was haunted.
They were starting without them.
The term "sick building syndrome" (SBS)

did not make the dinner guests angry.
Nor were they linked to time spent in a building.
The airport was haunted for five minutes.

Baggage bag, shoulder thing? Bag? Ready? Julia?
Crispy Ambulance was on the taxi cab radio.
Parkas teeming with goose down

adjusted themselves in the backseat: ".... Already critically acclaimed
for a number of youthful film roles," Crispy Ambulance said,
"... recall she was in the 2001 film about a white *mesquinesque*

Midwestern girl who moves to Chicago, where her new boyfriend is a black teen from the South Side with a rough, semi-autobiographical past."

Just for a Single Moment

The [female] *Golden Flint* unrolls with tight
discordance on the left ventricle for a full half-
minute before the guilty teens are killed.

Her voice has arrived: "Shall we kiss on the lips,
or unlock the tool set and mend the serpent?"
You can answer, "Sure."

Or shall I say that I'm sorry? That on any *other* day
I would have asked you to alter your hair with lavender,
honey and lemon rind trails. But not today.

10 Things I Know About Toronto for a Fact

This town is positioned in a way that hurts.
This town needs an enigma.
This town is much like haunted lasagna.
This town's real estate fonts are ghastly.
This town needs serious werewolf awareness and improvement.
The religious banter at Dundas Square needs dance-theatre choreography.
The sea gulls and pigeons on Yonge street are well overdue in their applications for liquor licenses.
The stripper's union and the writer's union should just get on with it and play charity basketball.
The David Miller band needs do only Prince covers.
The Julia Stiles Banquet Face-Fetish Club should up its meetings to three times a week.

According to Cindnall G. Peacock, the newly appointed general
counselor at Canadian Busking Inc., "the history of the regulation in
these changing times helps you know how you got here from there, but
more importantly, how to make change with changing chords, and we're
not talking pants."
Wall-to-Wall–Write-on-My-Wall-Delete

The Julia Stiles Banquet Face-Fetish Club

With exegesis-resistant mascara,
duly licensed to breathe,
O fang-toothed beauty,

you draw your words in,
the ones you slurped
in the evil trailer minutes earlier.

Your chest at half-mast,
your face regulated by physics,
when you read your poem aloud

never addressing meaning
anywhere, tears streaking down
your plate-face (like a glacier

smeared in pretty pink),
you looked like a runny pie.
And then the poem was over.

"Emily"

(directed by Geoffrey Pigeon)

1.

It's Canadian Music Week.

Sound bite:
> "It is very relevant in Canada today."

Visuals, in CHALKBOARD jagged fonts:
> "An affluent suburb"
> "EMILY"

I've been on set all morning in my plaid
Eddie *[born December 23, 1964 in Evanston, Illinois]* Vedder
outfit.

How do I feel?
Like I have won a contest no one entered.

I am remixing my property fetish and
writing my graffiti on the "bedroom" walls.

Over and over I write
Emily "Amadeus" Haines
on the bedroom floor.

The walls are yellow and pink.
I am bored and grey/black.

2.

My graffiti letters are being filled up by busy hands
in crayon n wax, or enamel spray-paint.
The same busy hands are pasting
samples of my 1992 High School

Greatest Literary Hits in the foreground.
In the background, a story about a spaceship
taking my father off our front lawn.
The pages are photocopied.

I live with cups of water
under the Emily stand-in's combat boot.
She is instructed to mimic a 17-year old
girl/boy at home drawing pictures
of combat babies—*"so bikinis and tanks,"* the director says.

She shrugs and rubs the crayon across the big page.
She's on her pink knees.
Her miniskirt calculates no shadow.
She's gesture drawing like crazy.

"With her on top!" Geoffrey yells,
telling Emily to draw her own likeness,
"or, you know, whatever you feel like."

3.

Conquering the tanks and planes,
she is my King Kong
with cadmium hair and short-skirted legs raised in a V.
She does a combative silver kick for an outtake.
Today is just like the day I heard
Emily of Metric ruined my world.
It's hard to cease thinking about it.

"Just walk around the room, like you're angry."

She is my King Kong.
I am her airplane glued incorrectly.
She may break a nail on my skull.

"Like your parents have just said you can't go to the biggest party of the year."

Dead disco bombs from her eyes
in soft, maroon tear drops.

Because I'm Eddie V. I sing:

> "Leslie didn't give attention
> to the fact that Queen Emily
> of Metric ruined his world!
> Emily spoke on set today!
> Emily spoke on set today!"

"Look down. Now up. Okay, good."

I sing about staring at her leather coat,
how she seemed a harmless little tawny twit,
how she unleashed a sea lion,
gnashed my heart with a sneer,
and stomped in the mild dust of my quest.

I sing about how she clocked me
near the craft table
with a surprise left,
and left my jaw blurting.

> "Queen Emily of Metric
> ruined my world!"

I am singing about her
so I can forget about her,
so I can erase her forever
from the monochrome Billboard.

Fabrication Land

"It's a very good escalator."
"Oh really?"
"We rely on it."

Are there any examples
of personal tragedy in this mall?

Yes:

A bear eating my ankle cables.
A branch crushing mannequin calves.
A foot in a mouth, and a splint in passing.
A forest clearing soaking up the blood.
Another booklet of those Golden Flint coupons.

Vinegar

Outside, a long blue tear slowly drops.
Clean rain has a pH value of about five point six.

By comparison, vinegar has a pH of three.
I am no longer a symbol in a dream but a wet

extraction clasped with pincers,
then dropped, white, in your palm.

Clockers

The objectifying sales agents could not possibly decorate their ornate name plates in time for lunch.

Thanks to strategic planning by the God of color, their deadline was saved by temp angels.

Wrong Way to Tinsel

The midnight trains are boarding, all at the ends.
We leave the stars to judge us. We are not going to drink.
We will not get sick over cucumber sandwiches.

The conductor yells: "Dollars! Money! Diamonds!"
In the movie of us, right now, we are jar-brain gray
and our feet are made of glass so we can't walk.

But we can sing: "I'll move to Tinsel, and escape this road.
I'd build my house with sorrow.
I'll leave my shadow, my fallen-behind one,

my baby's breath, I wouldn't lie about you–
I'm not that kind of escapee. I'll move to Tinsel,
and beat this fork-tongued road."

The Cashier Isn't Always This Slow

1.

The cashier isn't always this slow.

Don't get all in a fractal curve over it.
Don't map it out or solar calculate.

It isn't therapeutic to be annoying.
Heels over tiles over time.
Pockets have lint.

Gardens are trimmed by artillery.
Maybe for a torpedo it is therapeutic.
We are in line and you are suffocating.

You are plotting and fuming.
It's just waiting.
We are in line and you are suffocating.

2.

The cashier isn't always this slow.
You are thoughtful in your search for
Unconditional Eternity.

When we are material we lose our sense of relevance.
We are bashful torpedoes with a pervasive
desire for permanence at the cost of others.

We are therapeutic when we
expand beyond individuality
into divinity.

3.

When paper was replaced by plastic
the human body was allowed to express
its increase in emotional movement.

New goods were the new Gods.
Dictators paper cut housewives with magazines.
Although this was happening already in the 60s and 70s,

the romance of punk which gave freedom to express an
    individual spirit
through the body's natural limitations,
allowed us to be the tiger who painted its own ferocious
    stripes,

or the doctor with her own airport safety pin surgery,
or the alien with its own intelligence and rules
that differed from the rules of the concrete wall.

4.

Social behavioral images of beauty used to sell plenty of
soap detergent in post-war American grocery stores.
Mr. Dickens Darwin has no guilt or shame or politics,

just the desire to play drums
in a band while wearing hot pink lace,
and to write love poems to dolphins while wearing
    sweat bands.

After she divorced her millionaire husbands

Mrs. Brönte Austen saw a brutal tree.
But all you see is a slow cashier.

You do not appreciate why she is slow,
nor that her hands are not always so.

5.

The cashier isn't always this slow.
Echoing off the resonance of domed concert halls,
without the celluloid or photographic image, without the
accessibility of cassette tapes, individual expression was still

at the mercy of atomic divisions between spirit fantasy and
natural living manifestation. Then came the dreams and
   wishes
of our neon heart signs flickering important messages:

Lather
        Rinse
                Repeat

6.

The cashier isn't always this slow.
This one is better than the ones my husband buys.

A middle class, retail life doesn't turn me on.
It's just not my fantasy.

The lily, however, makes me cum
(when I am alone, by the way) for ages.

The smell intoxicates my pink room and then my
    throbbing pussy
and I always cum 16 times.

7.

The cashier isn't always this slow
As I cried and I screamed,
she made change in slow motion.

Flowers turn me on.
So does a little red sex demon
that crawls out of your pants
and sings Dean Martin to me.

She is printing the receipt.
No, the machine does that.
She is tearing.

8.

My father used to take us grocery shopping
and talk about women in the produce aisles.
He aped and double-chinned his way through apples and
    bananas
while my sister and I wished we could feel our own reality.

He pushed the metal cart towards the cashier.
He was the misery we wanted to escape.
He wouldn't quit the brutal exchanges.
He wouldn't try to help himself or eat a peach.

9.

The cashier isn't always this slow.
As a result of the delay, my aorta is connected to your stomach.
Your umbilical memory flows into my cervix.

My ovaries shower sperm like phosphorescent seeds
onto your shoulder blade shield plates.

To bide the time you braid my hair
into ribonucleic helixes
while I whisper alien prayers back to you.

10.

In 19 years he
will be fully disillusioned.

His entire life's landscape will be
one long eyebrow hair unkempt, without direction.

A full lawn of forgotten tingles will grow.
And we will still be here, waiting.

The cashier isn't always this slow.
I know. You've said that.

Who will look after him in his complete infibulations?
In which aisle do we find our solace?

If he was waiting here with us, there would be hope.
But instead we are biased against him.

He thinks that if he pours off the fat
from his fried food, that will correct the

mental effects of his social hibernation
and his unloved self.

II.

The cashier isn't always this slow.
She sniffs her hand; she rubs her forehead.

His face is the colour of an alcoholic orange.
He is no one's responsibility.

We will find him one day, too late,
buried beneath his lumber stack.

Maybe you feel so little like superman because you are
out of touch with the possibility of yourself as *the hero*.

Always looking for a mother,
you resent the beauty of your woman.

Maybe you are subject to extensive
powers beyond your slightest control.

Yes, I agree.
The cashier isn't always this slow.

"The 10 Things I Am Going to Eat off Your Plate."

1. Kinks in the dishwasher's hand.
2. Prunings from the dinner rush.
3. Kale, cumin, with terse noodles.
4. Dense cold lime soup.
5. Apron paw prints of talcum'd flour.
6 & 7. Curry paste tears dangled over chocolate fondue.
8. Mercury salad dressing.
9 & 10. Salt-'n'-pepper.

"It's 1880s Night. You Look like a Slut."

Grow up and blow me.
Paper cut me.
Pronounce a ticket and write it up.
Hypnotize the pigeons.

Memorize the history of your uniformed body.
Throw a Virgin Molotov Cocktail into my mouth.
Duck. Caress imaginary violin strings
along the phantom gumline of my sensitivity.

It's 1880s night. You look like a slut.
It's Halloween. I want to scream.

Squeeze me into horrible structures.
Pay attention to me in redeemable coupons.
Shower me with redeemable coupon attention.

It's 1880s night.
And she has fallen to the bottom of the sea.
And a guitar is playing at the top of the mountain.

I Have Eaten the Oil Painting Which You Left on My Wall
For Greer

Thrown From A Boat, oil on canvas 1982, (1/8 x 3/4 inches).
I'm just being normal.

And you have stained all my clothes,
trousers to tees.

Did you dye your hair? You look like an oil painting.
Yes I dyed my hair. I am now a blonde. A very *blonde.*

Thanks for talking to me, Oil Painting
Don't be so dramatic.

I'm just being normal. You are the one who is dramatic,
    Oil Painting.
You are being an imprinted pixie with ten teeth marks.

The painting has captured your eyes nicely.
Your Norman Rockwell complex(ion) serves us just right.

Small House

It frightens him *chirp*
to remember its tiny door.

Soggy boots far away.
Was the tiny door rusty or red painted? *tweet*

Either way, the cold walk. His winter coat
over pajamas. His purple hands dyed by juice,

and pneumonia. Breakfast, then to school.
The small house on his family's front lawn.

He lived in it. Did his homework,
tea, out the door. Into the small

chirp house on the front lawn, to sleep. *tweet*
All the sparrows were taking Polaroids.

chirp "Sew this in your stroller. *tweet chirp*
Sew this in your storyline." *tweet*

From age 2-5 his earthling's eardrum
didn't *chirp* distinguish his own voice from the rain. *chirp*

He still wonders about the tiny keys
in his diaper. *tweet*

It frightens him
to remember.   *chirp*

Part 3:
An Effort Which Does Not Pay

Smaller Narrative

left your bathing suit
slung over a rusty
bike now

[it's in] in the backseat
of my mom's car now
now this is the beginning

of a smaller narrative
about a rusty bicycle coming
to terms with how you left your

bathing suit slung over
this is the beginning of a smile
now it's in the backseat of my mom

's car now
left it slung red like our hearts
pied with silver flecked dark orange

our small and narrative land
rust is a bloody colour at times   .

burned orange, stale almonds
suffered in yellow torment
Even wore a dress, she said

to her interview but not the suit
the bathing suit remained like sleeping

chain mail vest medieval even
slung over a rusty

it's twisted crotch
and straps are part
of a smaller narrative
slung over a rusty

a slow dribbling balloon dead
with air slung over a rusty
finishing nail

biked apart
photographers were happy

slung over
bathing suits drying

in the quicksand sun
quicksand kept moist by partial

clouds with air slung over a rusty
bathing suit

So… you left your bathing suit slung over
a rusty bike, it's in the backseat of my
mom's car now.

The Evaluation of a Patient with Abdominal Pain by a Bus Driver

Fumigate recent memory glands: "You may no longer have to spend the usual week in bed if you catch the flu.

When taken within 30 hours of getting sick, a drug called Zanamivir can shorten the duration of Type A and Type B

flu from seven to four days. Zanamivir still needs FDA approval. Next stop, Montreal."

"I actually diagnosed someone on my bus and administered medication about a month ago: A Mexican girl who had broken

out in an itchy rash after eating Chinese food. I haven't had a chance to follow the case up."

Parsley

A Simile For Parsley=Sponge Grasshopper

A small green recording device on the snack table, which picks up every morsel
of dialogue is a simile for AstroTurf. AstroTurf is a source of great microphone truth
concealment.

"I cannot fasten the golden brooch on her dress, because she will not wear it."
"These are delicious."
"It is a toy, it cannot speak."
"It is not a toy, it is jewelry, quit embalming yourself."
"I can see the golden glint in her eye."

Something is in all our teeths.

Pelvic Mascara Marking

I used to spout off rivers of poetic justice, injustice and pain.
I used to tweak prophecies on the mountaintops of
    insubordination.
Now look at me, reduced to some serial alleyway vendor's
    reputation,
as I Captain Crunch my route through this brutal morning
    of indifference.

Damn the nutrition pirates!

The world is quite a frightening little place isn't it?
Or is it simply not?

Now I say, no more rules, only action and reaction.
Consequences are self-imposed by *le biggest freak.*
It's just the sort of New Aged brinkmanship I will not suffer.

I used to spout off rivers of poetic justice–a sort of lofty
    concept
at this point–and croaked utterances in the night that no one
    was supposed
to hear. I cultivated a dry eye duct and a sense of entitlement
    for renegotiation.

Now, it's so hot! It's a very damning time.
Now I am more like Rimbaud trying to keep his cool with a
    few glasses of water.
I am like Arthur Rimbaud knowing that if he were to write
    out his actual state of mind,

and have a physical, climate-based reaction to his mental state,

that the water would first turn blood red, then explode the decanter
into tiny shards. Something romantic is bound to happen soon.

But for now we're gagged into utter oblivion. This is just for now,
and it won't get this good again. I've harnessed for you a most volatile world
that the people like to fingerprint on. Prometheus is blushing in the bushes.

I only wish that I didn't have to die.

Thieves Like Us

Jean Genet sleeps on a long hard napkin rectangle
inking his dreams in moats and daggers.
He is fettered to memories gray-scaled and clammy
while ghastly shards of meek soup, stubs of bread
percolate. While
unnerving resemblances along the bars
shoot vertically and spray discretely.
Vertigo hangnails read his unfortunate palm.
This is the universe, this is love, he thinks,
in floral disarray.
Softly each day they remove a rotting page from his thin grip.
He dies again, aging liver spots cold on the dingy cusp,
and a crack in his plate pollinates and a tiny pencil
finds garrison parchment soiled and ready
to hold on, so tough on the cud.

Use Weasel Phrases Megan, It's Your Turn

We track in on a big man crying in his own barber clippings.
 He pulls
taut a snotty rag between two fingers. His daughter is
 hanging from

the neighbour's window sill or clothesline and is jimmying
 her way towards
the house and the room where the man is sobbing like
 a weak little mouse.

He wipes his tears and says: "In my attic here there
are two figures, both me. Seated with elbows resting on the

table, I trace these elbows in crayon. Then slowly
I cut out the edges of my shirt's terrible elbow.

I make the elbow lids into game pieces,
and the table into a board game.

My amputated follicles frame the legislation of this game.
Some of the barber clippings are stained with spots of cough
 syrup."

Megan trickles in from the window ledge: "What a beautiful
 TAN he has!"
Rolling the dice I scream.

At one time this game, you know, it had a theme of dictation,
praise and momentum.

The tree outside is an alien to me.
I hear what Megan has to say:

"Dad quit locking the door."

Werewolf Tumour

We are in our torment, in our fiery youth. A local werewolf's frayed placard reads:

Sik Wulf Cancer Spare Summ Change

Conversation rays reveal he was diagnosed with irrevocable fleas last Wednesday. He may have to have his testicles removed.

"I don't take chances, if they are cancerous fleas, they could spread."

This assessment arrives from the dirty sea of his mouth. He is too psychotic to be nostalgic, too vitriolic to be morbid, or else I mean, "... not to be...." Whichever, I am riveted.

From time to time he gets up and walks around with a convincing limp. He eats from a giant bulk bag. "It's mostly dried horsemeat and tofu. I like to mix up the political menu, even in these malignant times." I am nodding in horror.

"Maggots have more fun," he muses, breaking off a section of my face and chewing the hot foamy sweat residue of another horrible dream. "I hate sleeping now," he admits.

The daylight or tornado is a warm relief, he observes, "compared to the death sentence of unwanted memories that have been creating sick, high-budget sequels under my arms."

He cites his body betraying him: "My armpit hair grows

in my sleep and infiltrates the dyed-black popcorn."

He speaks of his loss in the arena of love: "Everything resembles a night of swirls of red and black, then becomes a clean green field where my wolfen Julia and her new foxy dream man like to go. He and Julia are together, and I'm just a juvenile version of myself who can't find his bicycle."

Sorry, I try to say. I do some shaking of my head. He continues: "Everything is thematically a stain, a big uneven yellow and red stain on a bright white T-shirt. Julia is some inflatable cartoon long gone, OR, is she (am I?) the smell of fresh cut grass fingering her under a discontinued sunflower pattern 348 summer dress. How can anyone really know for sure?"

Politely, I excuse myself, collecting bits of my face from the dirty sea of his mouth
and the hollows of his outstretched claws, discreetly.

That's My Brother, Jawa

Did I have a sister? As a kid. Only as a kid. Holly helped me, forced

other kids on the street to eat a series of insects in water under the stairs.

She liked skater boys, she had long bangs and a series of clothes that were laundered next

to mine. I erotically filmed her friends baking cookies in their pajamas with my

pubescent Jawa eyes. Yellow eyes for a yellowing life. Fangs, I left them in the utensil drawer.

I watched them chew with braced teeth. But she, my

sister,

she was perfect: A knife through an orange. I was thermal rash: always came in first.

The difficult Bronchitis 400.

Arugula Wasted

I.

3:17 a.m., dressed in yellow bought from an ounce of sun,
            in green acquired from geranium leaves
my sister Arugula needs time to help heal her scabs.
The sun has been teething on her body.
"Eat your omelet psychopath!"
Yes Arugula is wasted. Her evening was a high-
octane liquor-chasing skirt twirling, thong-twisting
parade of odorous debauchery. The kind that is so often
    the source
of her sore disaster, comet scars and shredded nylons.
Yes, Arugula is wasted, my disaster

tart of a sister. Plucked remorseful from the cab's guts.
"She stinks!" I cried, paid the cab. As she
sleeps I whisper to journals, to tap-streams, out the scarred
    window,
into the bulging evening. "I haven't seen our parents in
    years. Not
since the birch trees were full of leaves and swallows."
The giant armadillo-shaped leaves that clung to our birch tree
were a tambourine in the rain, the swallows a twittering choir.
"You are a hung-over, slutty hand glider," I say.

The rainfall of truth has been delayed.

2.

I must help her get to the door. In a malicious dream sequence
with tinfoil sun squinting, she is listening to vodka-thinning storylines.
She clubs the bouncer in the noggin with Flint's ceremonial mask, hard
gold leaf edge finish, seventy-nine ounces, leather strap incl.

The bouncer is sweating gold and blood. The bartender calls her *Rocket,*
slang for Arugula. My cauldron-eyed sister deploys her evil nose
across razored drugs, and swallows spiked cold drinks all night at Wrongbar.
Hair, natty. Skin, sore.   Merlot underwear worn-thin.

The back of her neck is knotted in pie-bite (blueberry)-sized bruises
as phantom men continue teething,   on and on.

To heal her baby Arugula sister born in May, I, Poltergeist [older by
seventeen months] tuck my heart into a clamshell and log data dutifully.

3.

I log data dutifully   while Arugula in her pupa state
(i.e. caked blood on her wrists and blouse collar, runs in
her stocks full of comet scars) is crawling around chatting
up sick parasites.
How tough it's going to scrub washed vomit, farmer's
grease and the dirty pollen of last night out of her sick
skirt. The stink clings hard and stiff and gritty and appears
to be lime coloured.

Outside, the last silver leaf is falling from our birch tree so
slowly that it hurts to watch.
It will be another seven years before the tree makes sound
again in the rain.

Acknowledgements

I wish to thank Jason Camlot for his careful guidance, and to the magazines that supported some of these poems along the way, including *Existere, Nth Position,* and *Prism International.* Thanks also to *Broken Pencil, Open Book Toronto,* Kerry, Jennifer, Angela, Mary, Karen, and my family.

Dubbed a "Toronto small press fixture" by *Flare Magazine* in 2005, Nathaniel G. Moore is the author of the humour book *Bowlbrawl,* the Catullus-infused novel-in-poems *Let's Pretend We Never Met,* and the teen-psychodrama-noir novel *Wrong Bar.* He is an editor at *Broken Pencil* magazine and a columnist for *Open Book* Toronto. From 2004-2009 he has served as an editor for *Danforth Review.*